Jo's Book of Birds For Kids

Josephine Gerweck

Avi + Amba –

I work with your Father he is a wonderful Doctor but more importantly A very kind man. Have fun reading with your parents soon you will know your ABC's And all the birds. Enjoy the great outdoors!

♡ Josephine

PAGE PUBLISHING, INC.
Conneaut Lake, PA

First originally published by Page Publishing 2019

ISBN 978-1-64628-549-5 (pbk)
ISBN 978-1-64628-553-2 (digital)

Printed in the United States of America

Dedication

Dr. W. William Byrnes, my father. He instilled in me a love of birding and nature.

Mrs. Barbara Gerweck, my mother-in-law. Her encouragement
and support inspired me to create this book.

Donald Munson, my neighbor and friend. He encouraged
me to draw and to enjoy the creative process.

 **A** *is for* *AVOCET*

Who lives by the sea

I eat shrimp and do not like cold water

1

B is for BLUEBIRD
As blue as can be

I live near open fields and sit on tree branches

2

C is for CARDINAL
So red it's a winner

I visit bird feeders and love pine trees

3

D *is for* *DUCK*
That dives for its dinner

I live in ponds, marshes, rivers, and lakes

E *is for* *EGRET*

Stands still in the reeds

I live in fresh water and salt water marshes

F is for *FOX SPARROW*

Hunts in leaves for some seeds

I live in forests and look for food under leaves

G *is for* *GOLD FINCH*

In summer turns yellow

I live in bushes and eat flower seeds

7

H *is for* *HUMMING BIRD*

A fast flying fellow

I visit gardens with colorful flowers

is for **INDIGO BUNTING**

With color so bold

I live in farmland, eating seeds and insects

9

J *is for* *JUNCO*

Who arrives when it's cold

I live in forests, and visit parks and gardens

K is for *KING FISHER*

Perched looking for fish

I live near lakes, rivers, and ponds

11

L is for *LOON*

Diving deep with a swish

I live on lakes and on the ocean.

M

is for *MOURNING DOVE*

Cooing all around town

I live in open fields, on lawns, and under bird feeders

N is for NUTHATCH

That climbs upside down

I live in pine trees and forests

O *is for* OWL

They "hoot" when they speak

I live in wooded areas and hoot at night

P is for PUFFIN
With a colorful beak

I live near the ocean on rocky shores and islands

16

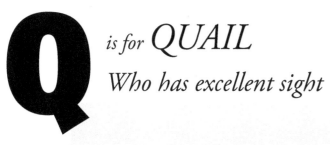

Q *is for* **QUAIL**
Who has excellent sight

I live in deserts and dry grasslands

17

R *is for* *RED-TAILED HAWK*
That soars like a kite

I live in trees near open fields, perching on branches

**S** *is for* *SONG SPARROW*

Who sings until dark

I live in thickets, pastures, and gardens

19

T *is for* *TUFTED TITMOUSE*

Hiding food in tree bark

I live in woodlands, parks, and shade trees

**U** *is for* *UPLAND SANDPIPER*

Who hides in plain sight

I live in open fields and farmlands

21

 *is for* **VIREO**

Eyes circled in white

I live in forests, parks, and visit bird feeders

W *is for* *WREN*
That's singing for hours

I live in parks, farms, and backyards

X *is for* XANTHUS'S HUMMINGBIRD
Sipping nectar from flowers

I live in Mexico and find nectar in colorful plants

Y is for *YELLOW WARBLER*

That's a brilliant yellow

I live in bushes near streams, feeding on insects

25

Z *is for* *ZEBRA FINCH*

A faraway fellow

I live in Australia, eating seeds and fruit

About the Authors/Illustrators
Creative Profiles

Josephine Gerweck is a registered nurse in critical care. She served as a Navy lieutenant in a Fleet Hospital in Saudi Arabia during Operation Desert Storm. She lives with her husband in Western Massachusetts. They have two grown sons, and she has seven brothers and sisters. Her love of birds and the outdoors was instilled in her by her late father, Dr. W. William Byrnes. They went on many bird walks together throughout New England.

Thomas Gerweck works with retirement plans in the financial industry. An avid reader, he enjoys playing tennis and hockey. His late father-in-law always recognized his ability to "spot birds" in the wild.

Donald E. Munson is an artist with works in multiple museum collections. He worked as a publishing art director and college educator in New York and Massachusetts. He was passionate about guiding this project, overviewing every step of the process.

CPSIA information can be obtained
at www.ICGtesting.com
Printed in the USA
BVHW021226070522
636175BV00002B/3